GOLDEN TIME GATES
BOOK OF ART

SANTO CERVELLO

The New Art Renaissance

The Golden Time Gates Collection of Five Volumes of Art by Santo Cervello; hold more than 600 wonderful images that are now available to view and to purchase around the world. "The New Art Renaissance," quietly seeds itself to grow and to share its powerful story of past, present, and future time. Millions of young artists worldwide are quietly working, and reflecting, creating and telling their truth. The ancient art books sealed in rooms of stone are granted permission to speak. "I am the earth. I am the water of the sea. I am the fire of your mind. I am the wind. Get to know me before you fly away to some distant universe." The Earth speaks. Is all this not true?

Charleston, SC
www.PalmettoPublishing.com

Time Gates: Volumes III and IV

First Edition

Hardcover ISBN: 978-1-68515-720-3

Paperback ISBN: 978-1-68515-721-0

eBook ISBN: 979-8-88590-121-5

ACTORSCORNERCAFE.COM

A special thanks to Grace Lebecka who has focused her time to work for the highest possible good. Her contribution to the book is appreciated.

Sound Engineer

Earth sound

Music from the distant knowing

String

Vibrations amplified

Life and death

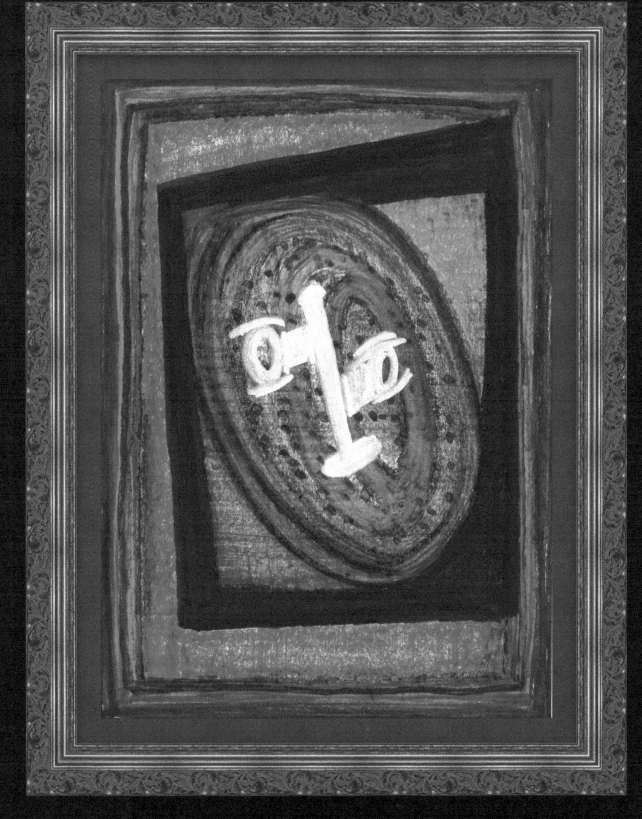

TIME GATES

THE INTUITIVE ART OF SANTO CERVELLO

VOLUME 3

SANTO CERVELLO

FOREWORD

by Grace Lebecka

Here is another powerful volume of "Time Gates, The Intuitive Art of Santo Cervello" Volume 3. Are you ready for a wonderful ride? The Sound Seeker's Journey becomes akin to a possible reality shift of peace on Earth.

A few years ago, we received a wonderful visit from our dearest friends. John and his wife drove up from Malibu, California to the Santa Ynez Valley and joined us for dinner. John is a kind and gentle fellow. He works as a music producer and loves to create clean, clear, wonderful sound for his musician clients. The music touches people around the world.

Santo spent some time with John, asking him one question: Is it possible to find the crystal clear sound that creates peace for humanity on Earth?

The book is full of wandering detours, tests, entrapments, real dangers and exciting encounters. There are healers and guides who bring hope to humanity with a slice of Johnny's apple pie.

Are Time Gates portals within all of us that we need to cross, overcoming and slaying the dragon of our own indifference? Can we find peace that gives hope to the hiding child in the Time Gates of our heart? Enjoy.

CONTENTS

GOLDEN TIME GATES
BOOK OF ART

By Santo Cervello

Before a child is born, the beating of its mother's heart is its home. Later, the child learns about the wind, the mountains, the oceans and the stars. We can trace the sounds of goodness from the outer web and into the inner thread to be amplified for the peace of our children. Yes, there is the roar of the wind and the sea. There is the roar of mountains and trees. There are roars of hunger, of sickness and of rage. The silent sound of the wind will guide us to a gentle field where there is peace and no need to slay the dragons. The Actor enters reading "The Art Book Play".

Sound Engineer

Born To Be Free

Sound Seeker

Dancing On A String

Clear Waters

Music Rooms

CERVELLO
2013

Planet Sing

Injectors Wheel

Vibrations

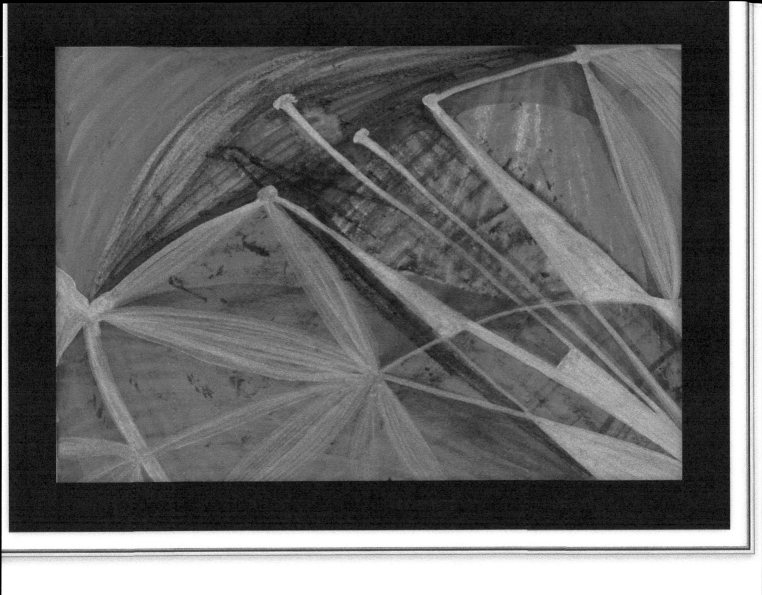

Orbs Understanding

The Pyramid Sea

Memory Store

Space Bridge

Love's Dream

Sun People

Healer's Call

Blue Bird Sleeps

Whistling Stone

ACTOR SPEAKS–LIFE IS CREATED BY LOVE'S DREAM

"A Dinner Story" from the Actor's Corner Café. To celebrate Father's Day, Honey and Michael with his parents requested a special seat in the courtyard beside the fountain. The waiter easily accommodated their wishes.

In the middle of dinner, Michael came up to the waiter and said: "in a minute I am going to propose to my girlfriend, in front of my parents. Here is my cell phone – please, record every moment. It is a surprise. Now I am going to get the flowers from the car. They think it's for my Dad."

The waiter got so excited! In whispers he told everyone inside the Café about the surprise. Then he ran into the kitchen with Michael's phone in his hand to tell the chef there was going to be a proposal.

WAITER

"Oh my gosh. Oh my gosh. Should we open up the champagne?"

ACTOR

The waiter was so nervous and excited for the couple.

WAITER

"Can you open the champagne for Michael now? He is going to propose."

ACTOR

Michael came from the car holding a bouquet of red roses in hand. With a serious smile on his face he zeroed in on his girl Honey. Everyone in the restaurant got it. It was happening!

WAITER

"This is a moment of the century."

ACTOR

Michael kneels in front of Honey. Honey screams, everyone is frozen, and it is all recorded by the waiter, on the iPhone.

Michael places his hand inside the red rose bouquet and brings out a golden diamond ring. Michael asks Honey if she will be his wife. Everyone has tears in their eyes.

The champagne bottle was opened with the entire restaurant bubbling with joy. Everyone giving Michael and Honey sparkles of congratulations.

They all raise their glasses of wine with cheers and applause. Thank you, Honey. Thank you, Michael – for sharing your wonderful Father's Day gift. The Old Priest enters and sits beside the young couple.

OLD PRIEST

On what roads have men and women traveled?

In what season did we journey together?

Do we plow the fertile fields?

Do we give our hearts to the rich black earth

only later to abandon the land?

We the travelers, cross each other's paths

to meet for one magnificent moment.

ACTOR

"Have you discovered the sound that creates World Peace?" asks the Priest.

The new moon shines deep and gentle over the castle roof.

Some travelers come here to remember

those moments shared with their loved ones.

Others come for their first experience.

On a warm summer evening people

often walk to the café from their Hotels.

They listen to the sound of water

touching the fountain stones.

There are sounds of owls, (Owl sound)

and the whistle of the ancient bird lingers in the summer mist.

Guardian's Of The Egg

One Body Many Souls

Lovers On The Swing

Lost Lands

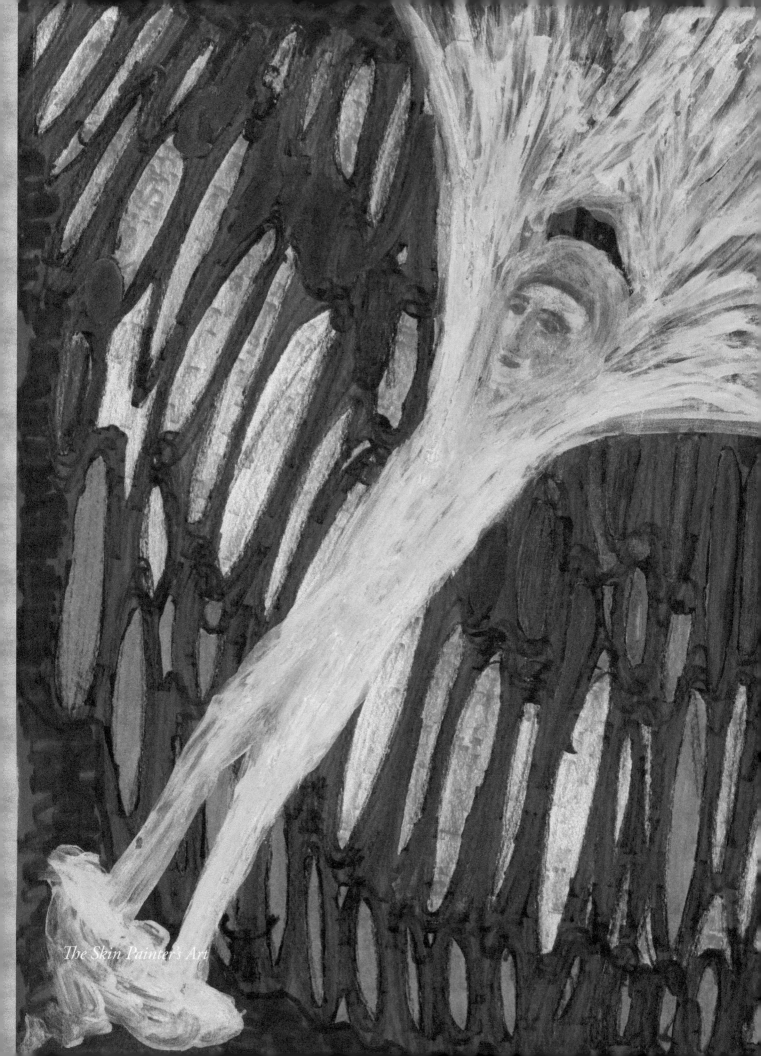

The Skin Painter

The Giant's Family

Born Free

The Lord's Car

War Slave

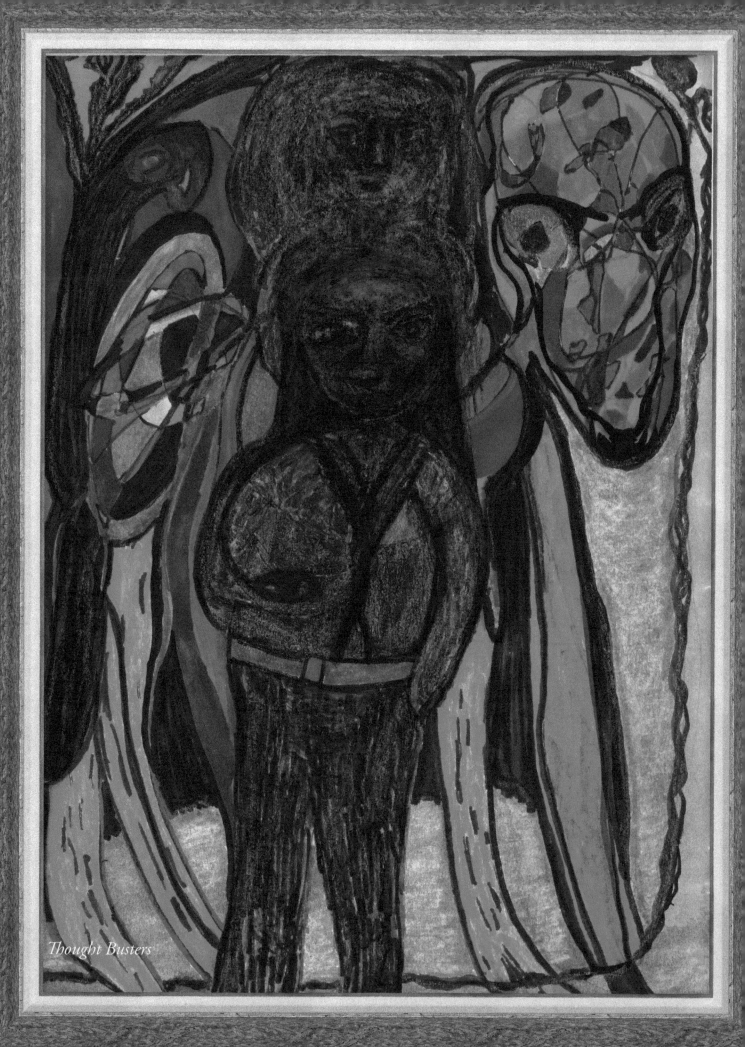

Thought Busters

Bubble Workers

First King

ACTOR

It was a dark night outside in the hiding and hushed-up lands of dark places where the encoders live. No one talks or writes about the encoders in the news. It must not be written. A powerful voice encoded the thinking and a world power sealed its place.

Energy always moves and changes but not like water or like clocks keeping time. The people march, keeping time in step throughout our cities, towns and lands. Inner spaces were opened up that should have remained closed.

I am trying to say something clean and good and fires come to mind. Months before the sparks were lit there was such anger and hunger and tension. Who lit the fires? Then the rain came and the explosions and the flood of mud and boulders and people losing their lives and their homes. The invasion of everything was planned and set on fire by the wind and electrical wires.

Some people who lost their homes came to dine at the restaurant. I remember a lovely couple whose house was miraculously left intact. Some neighbors lost everything.

A neighbor was interviewed on the local TV Station.

Looking straight into the camera she said, "the first thing each morning I would greet my neighbors and their children going to school or to work and now they are all gone. The whole family is gone. Get to know your neighbors, please. Get to know them. "

Underground Lords

CERVELO

Second King

Chief Dan George

Wired Up

Sound Heals

The House

Thieves

A Friend

Aliens' Gate

The Hospital

The Truth

The Lie

Broken Trust

Bike Ride

The Doctor

Jupiter To Earth

The Ice Landers

The Navigator

Forbidden Room

Picture On The Wall

Global Pandemic

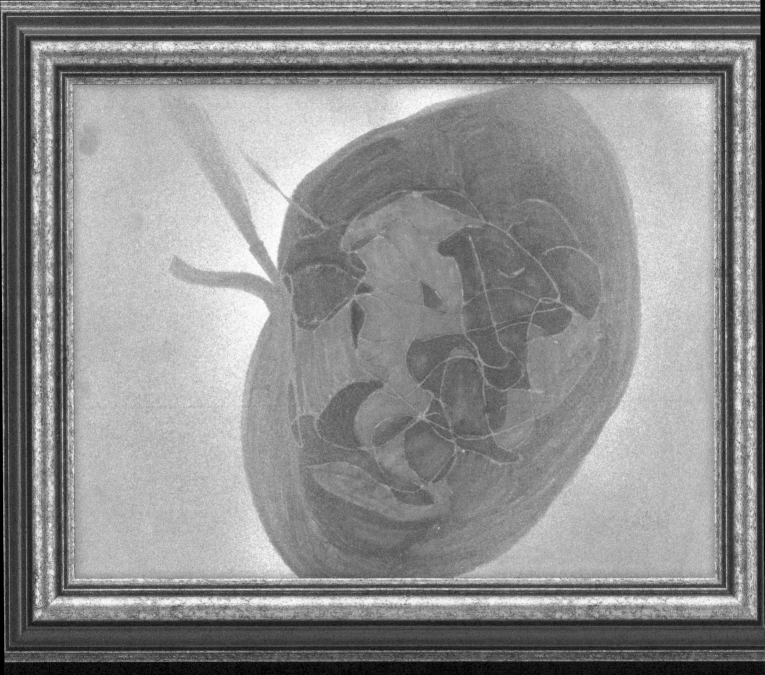

The Seed

The Professor

Flowers In The Hall

Hotel Unknown

Fire Queen

Johnny Apple Seed

Cash Man

The Gardener

The Farmers

Holding Space

Black Elk Speaks

Graduation Day

Art Sale

Dream Catchers

Watchers

The Takers

Chief Dan George

Peace Arch

Medicine King

Walking Tower Motel

The Judge

A Child Is Born

Gathering Jewels

The Temple

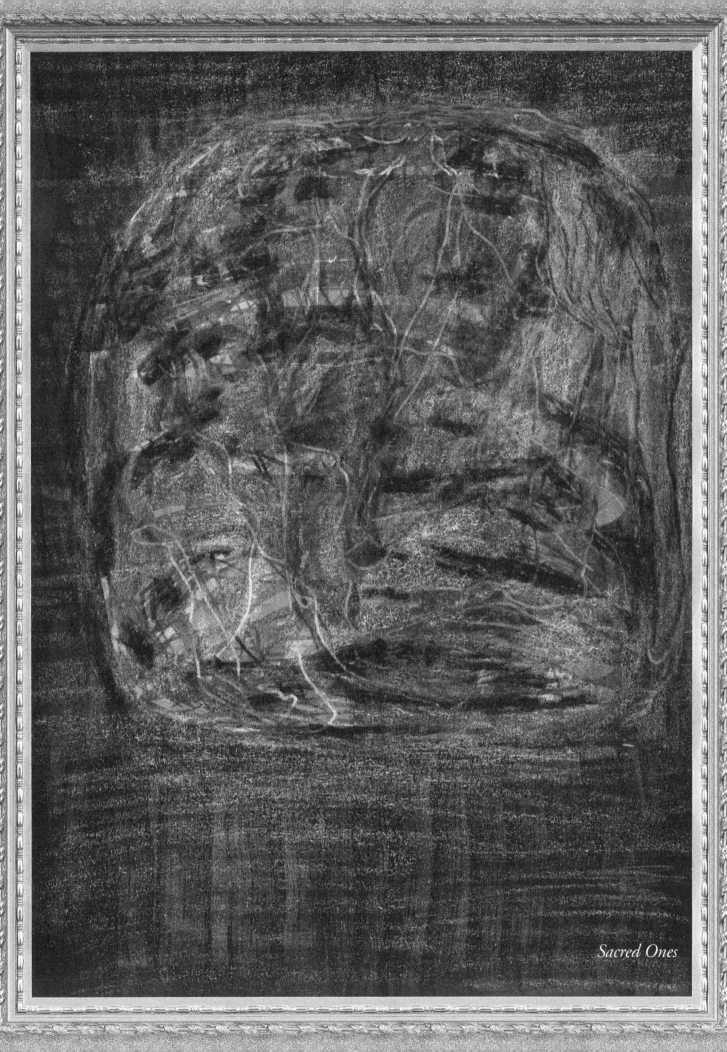

Sacred Ones

Put Your Green Skirt ON

Mary Queen OF Scots

The Old Sun King

Earth

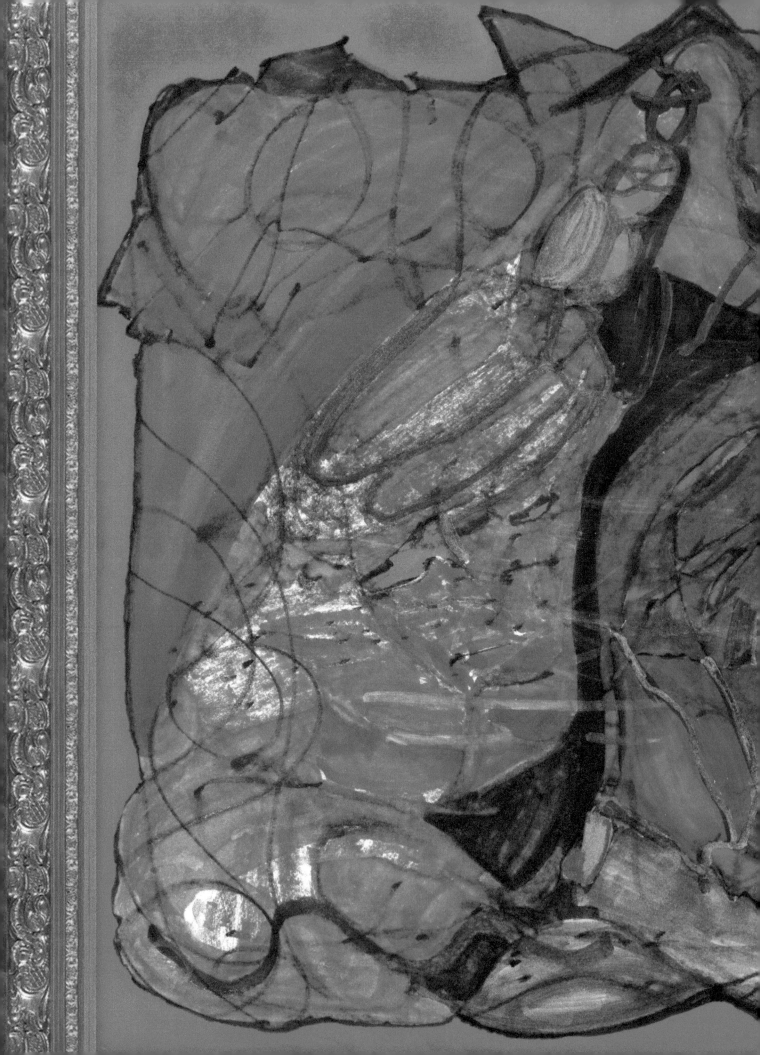

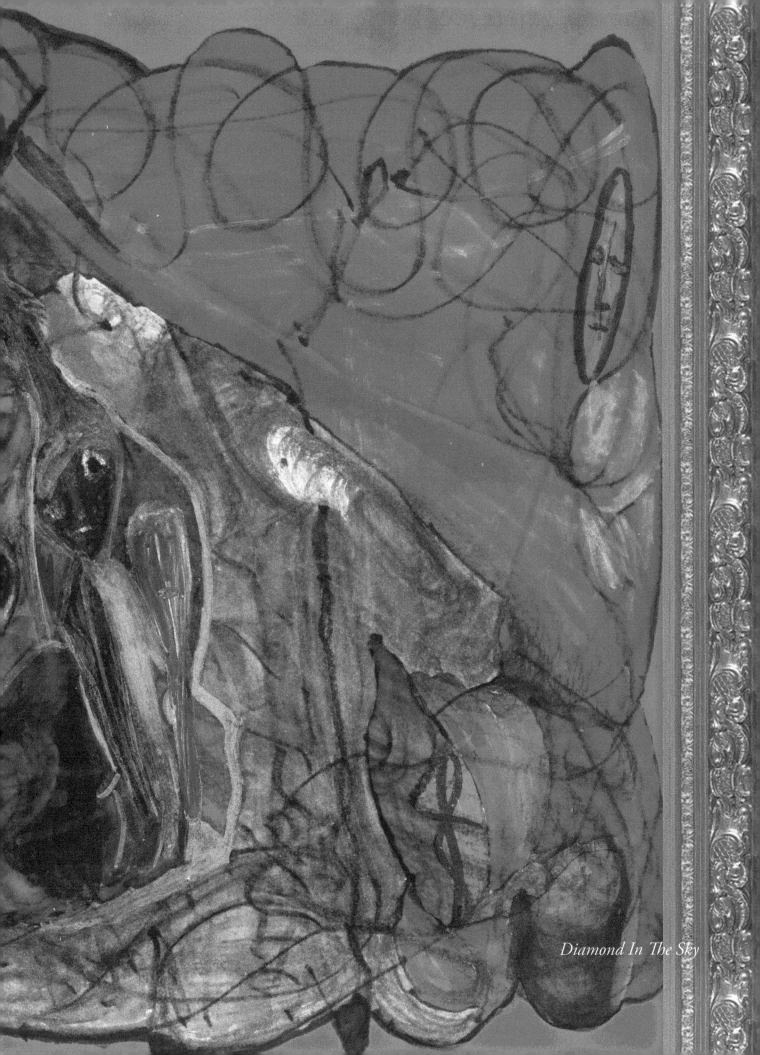

Diamond In The Sky

Present, Past, Future

War

ACTOR

Behind a closed door a small child is hiding. From the other side of the door, she asks an honest question. "What is your name?" I ask her. "I am Jane", she says.

JANE

Where are the Sound Seekers, Governments of the World, Kings and Queens, NASA, The Pope, The United Nations. All People on Earth, why don't they find the Peace Note? NASA traveled to Mars and they can't find a note that creates world peace?

ACTOR

There was a big long pause here. The note will be found, and the sound will be heard and there will be Peace on Earth.

JANE

People can't make money finding a peace note.

ACTOR

I hope you're wrong, Jane.

JANE

Me too.

The Purple People Are Here

The Flowers Are Back

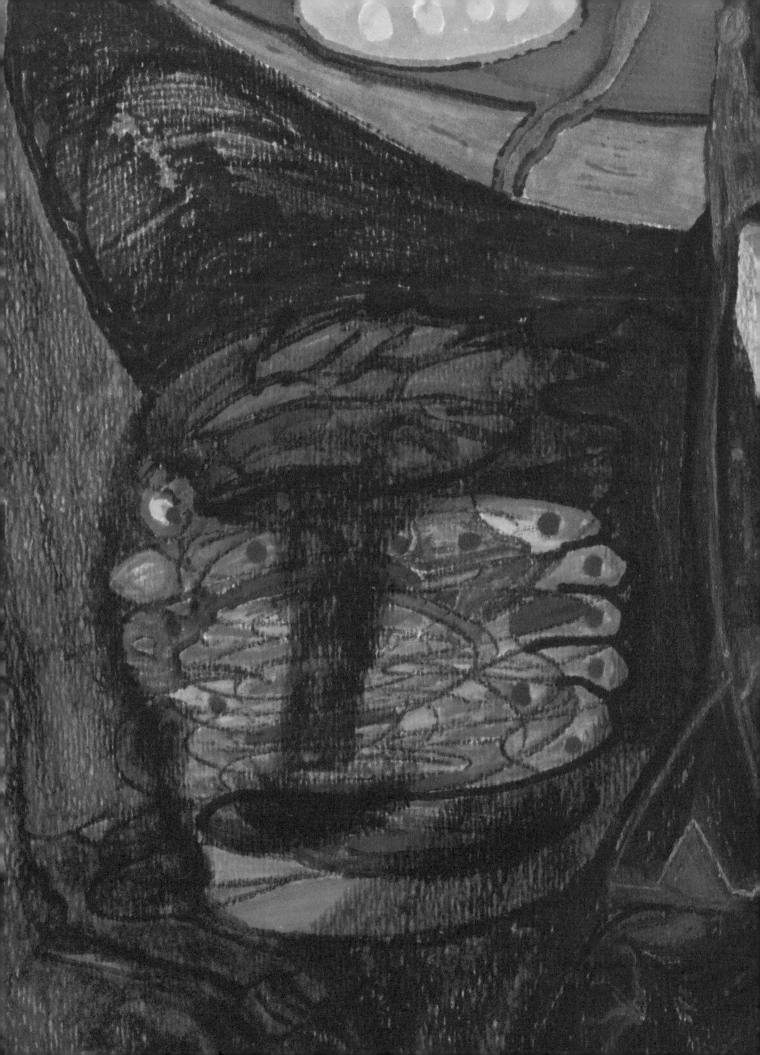

Hunger Hunger Why

Web Creator

Tricksters

Stop The War

Pretenders

Silence

Lord's Car

Searching

Shifter In The Stream

Window Dreams

A Link

Colors

Traversing Space

Silver Coils

The Cave

The Centre

Three Friends

The Composer

Pools of Music

Broken Stairs

Flying Carpets

Stain Glass

The Hill House

Soldiers Return Home

The Barn Window

Jungle Roots

The Monkey Tree

The Jungle Spirit

Growing Space

Moon Beam

Soul Food

The Hands

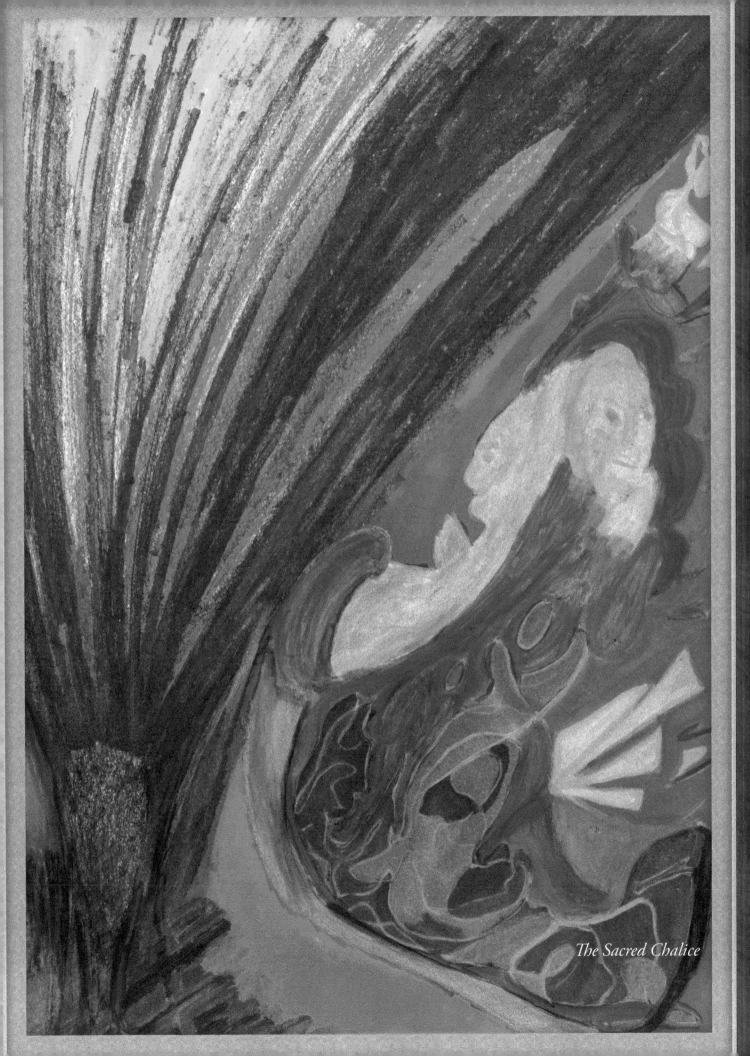

The Sacred Chalice

Golden Light

LUTEOLIN

Recorded Prayer

Palace Of The King

The Marriage

Jane Walker's Garden

The Seeding

The Healing

The Queen's Dream

The Mask

Open Door

A lost key opens the ancient computer room door. The computer is incased in stone, within a safe. The safe is kept inside a storage bin full of sand. The People are uploaded, as they enter the room, then computerized, and encoded. The alignment and vibration of the body sound within each person's spirit is kept hidden but never forgotten or lost. The Old Priest has entered Jane Walker's Garden.

Dancer In A Frame

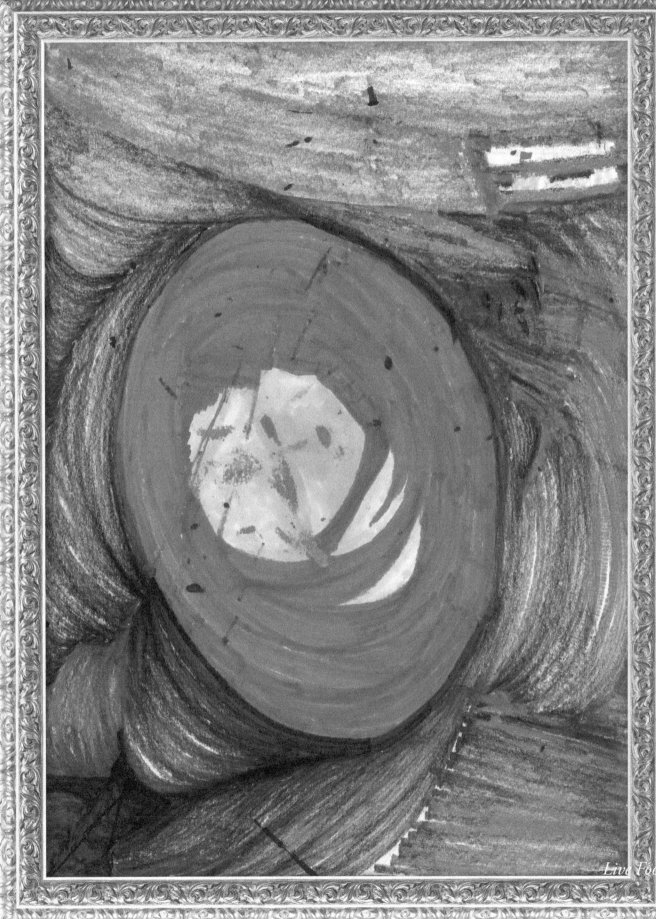

Live Food

Tree Talking

The Gardener

The Listeners

Body Alignment

Alone In The Grass

The Lion Never Sleeps

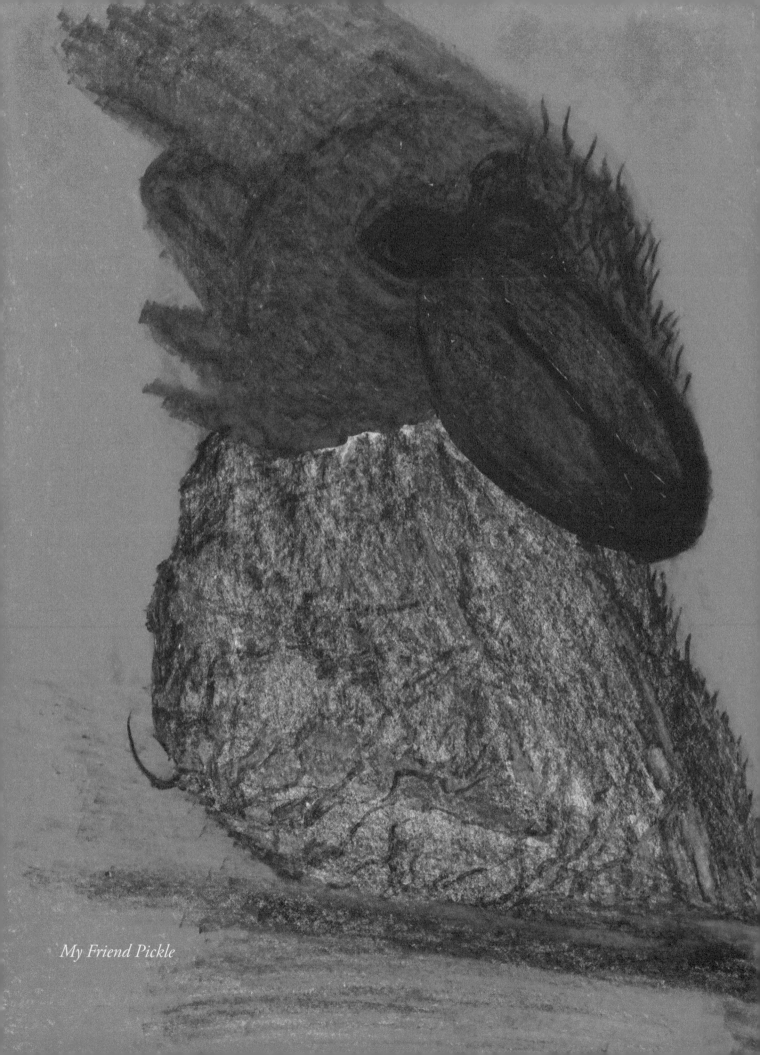

My Friend Pickle

The Path Finder

EPILOGUE

Epilogue by Santo Cervello

Sound vibrations hold our body and life in place. The outer web is the aura of our body which holds the emotions. The aura also holds the thoughts that travel into our physical body through our inner threads and into our nervous system to the brain. We already Know this.

Eight people stand on a tiny musical thread. A guitar string will snap if it is too tight. That is the way it is. What are we to do? Thank you for being on this journey of Time Gates Volume 3.

Golden Time Gates

As I paint and draw, I'm listening to the
Earth. I don't know how the images
will evolve when finished or if it will be art.

The Earth is becoming reborn.

Permafrost is melting and

Methane Gas is rising.

Huge sinkholes appear worldwide.

The Earth is gentle and yet fierce.

Six billion people who live on our Earth
know something is happening.

I hope you are well and I thank you for being
on this golden journey of "Time Gates."

TIME GATES

THE INTUITIVE ART OF SANTO CERVELLO

VOLUME 4

SANTO CERVELLO

The Cathedral

CONTENTS

I dedicate my life to the ancient Law

Of cause and effect through sound

FOREWORD

NEW ART RENAISSANCE "TIME GATES" VOLUME IV
by Grace Lebecka

Santo asked me again to write a foreword. He said the golden book combining volumes III and IV is about defining the sound for World Peace. According to this volume, the sound of peace on Earth has been found and amplified.

The special quality about Santo's art is that it takes you within, to the inner chambers of your own being. This time I concentrated solely on the sense of hearing. While I was going inside these images, I put on an amplifier to my ears and listened.

Surprisingly, I could actually hear the forces of nature, the splashing rivers, and the roaring waves of ocean currents along with other noises. These sounds I call 'metallic intersections'. The art images created in the year 2020/2021 are the reflecting mirrors of wind, fire and space, echoing the voices and disturbances of our world.

There are swarms of sounds striving to overpower each other, struggling to be heard. Shrieking noises of anger and destruction, closely followed by whispering voices of persistent calmness and compassion.

Santo takes his audience into another journey of the Sound Seeker. Again, as in the previous volumes, we stumble upon the realms of Below and Above - we find ourselves sinking into the abyss and, before long, soaring into deep cosmic space. Here we encounter various characters, and meet the forces of cosmos and nature all connected to vibrations of amplified fields. Through Santo's art, we can hear the silence of snowflakes falling, the singing of a mountain bird and the sound of a red rose growing in Jane Walker's garden.

It is the hero's journey of the Sound Seeker who, passing through the Kingdoms of the Queen, of the Lords of the Underworld and of heaven, plunging into the deep waters and the space of earth, arrives and defines the sound vibration of Peace for the world.

INTRODUCTION

By Santo Cervello

Humanity seeks the truth and our hidden world of history is released. The museum doors which had been sealed <u>are now open</u> to reveal the reality of the Time Gates. The truth stops the never-ending stories.

Computerized Cathedrals and the Memory Chips. Electrified people, living from the Past, Present and Future, now hearing a sound never heard. There is the master's child, there are flowers and old mirrors, and the art renaissance. There are songs of joy and there's a time when a little girl was born. The Emperor and Queen seemed to be dancing inside the Great Pyramid of Giza.

I remember sitting on the floor of <u>the Birth Canal waiting to enter</u> the Queen's Chamber. There was a sound, reaching out to be heard. The lost keys were found in those rooms, by the circles that never sleep; always in space, always awake, born again and again. The sound engineer will tell the story, how he amplified the note of Peace that belongs to the Earth. The chattering sounds of War are heard no more.

Computerized Cathedral

Communicators

Philadelphia Experiment 2021

Stepping Down

Body Shifter

Memory Chip

Sky Fighter

Hearing Sound Never Heard

Controllers

Space Benders

The Priest

The Chant

The Shield

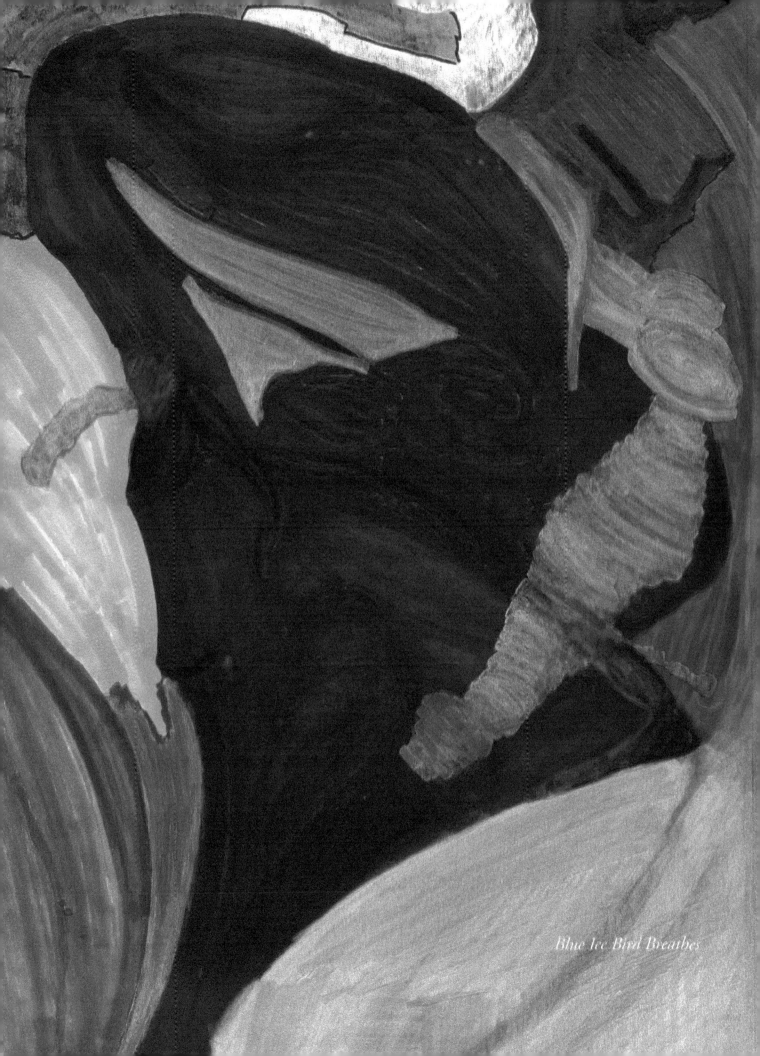

Blue Ice Bird Breathes

Sky Mountain

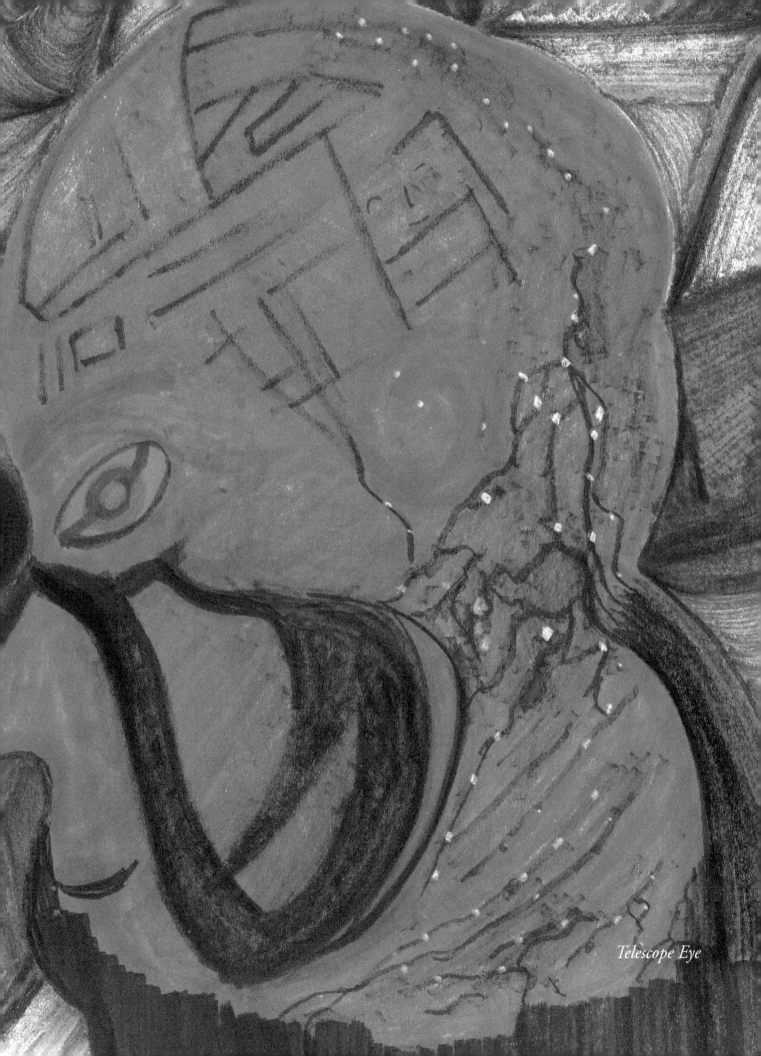
Telescope Eye

Wearing Silken Threads

Blue Heart

The Master's Child

Window Cleaner

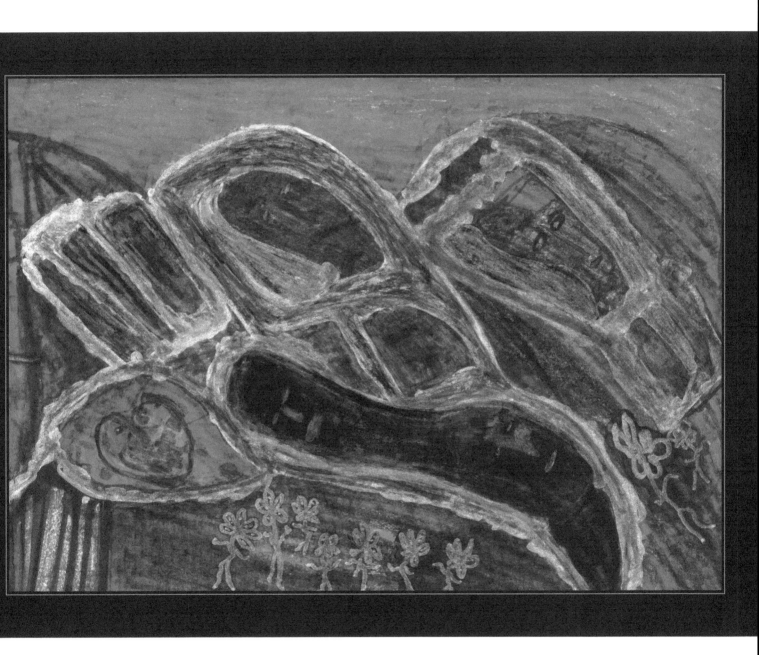

Flowers & Old Mirrors

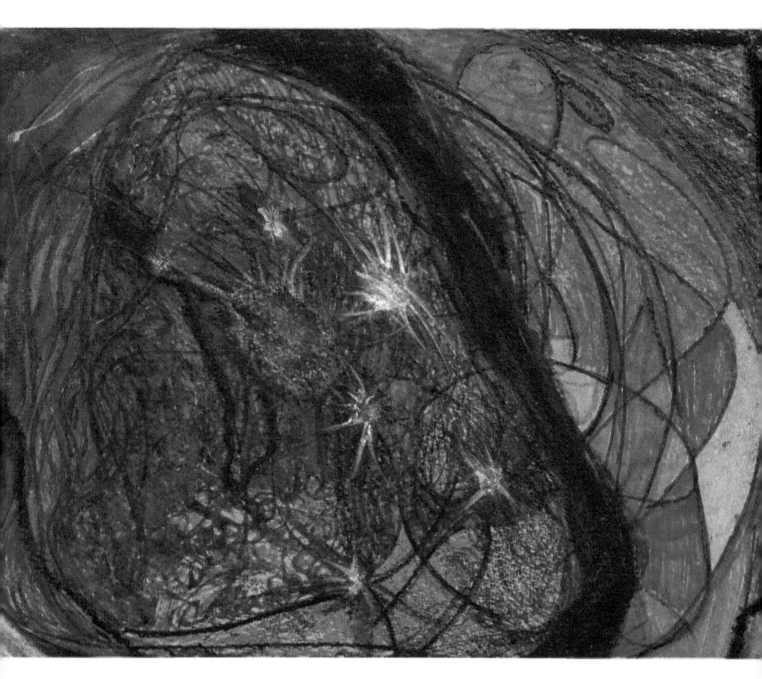

Healer's Stone

A Friend

Art Renaissance

Song Of Joy

Purple People

Jane Walker's Rose

Jane Walker – A time when a little girl was born and her mother died. "A moment to build a garden for my mother," she said. When Jane Walker grew up she created a garden not far from the White House.

The President

The Music

Volcano's King

Mountain Side

Space Flights

Love Seats

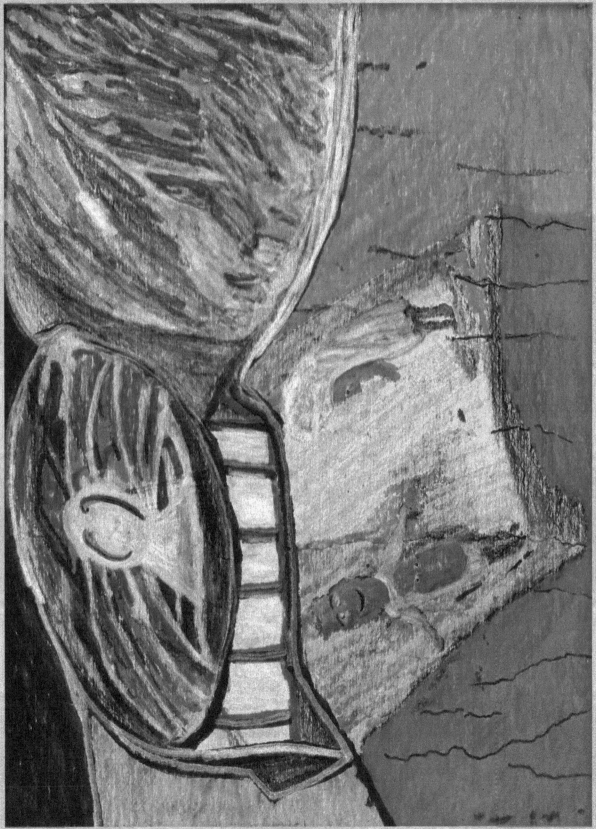

The Reader

Bird's Nest

Child Waiting

Returned From Mars

Thief One

Thief Two

Storms At Home

Ships Adrift

Close All Hatches

Stand Ready

Time Gate Runner

Frog Sanctuary

I'm No Frog

I am Cat

Encoding Egypt

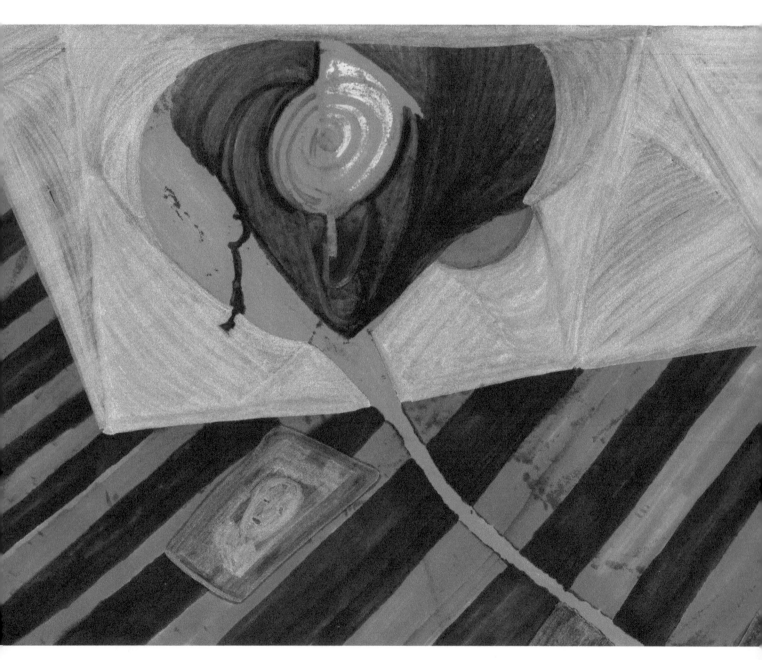

Reborn From Melting Snow

Jane Walker's Garden

Horse Riding

Hold Peace Within

Earth Seekers

Form Builders

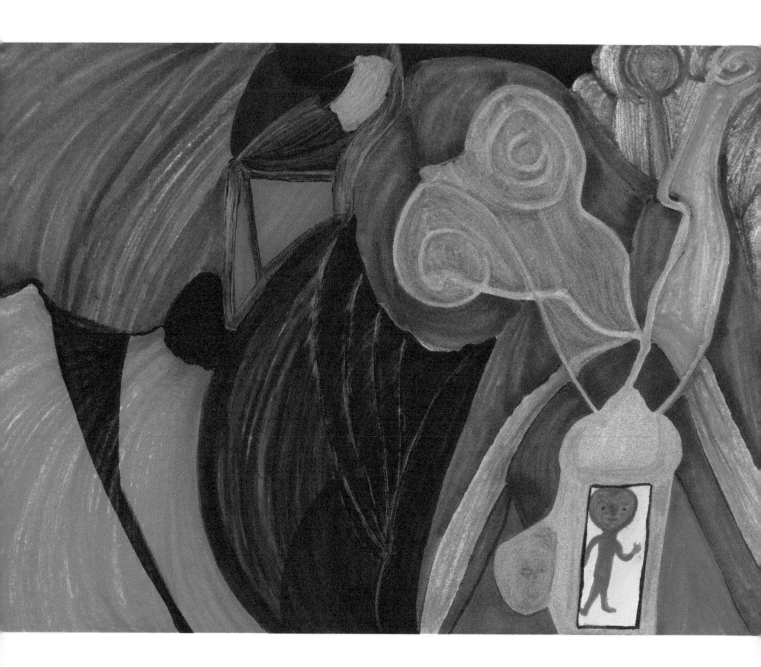

Computer Mouse

The Gathering

Sound Tracer

The Recording

This Way Up

Bird Feeder

The Abyss

Bird Song

Bubbles

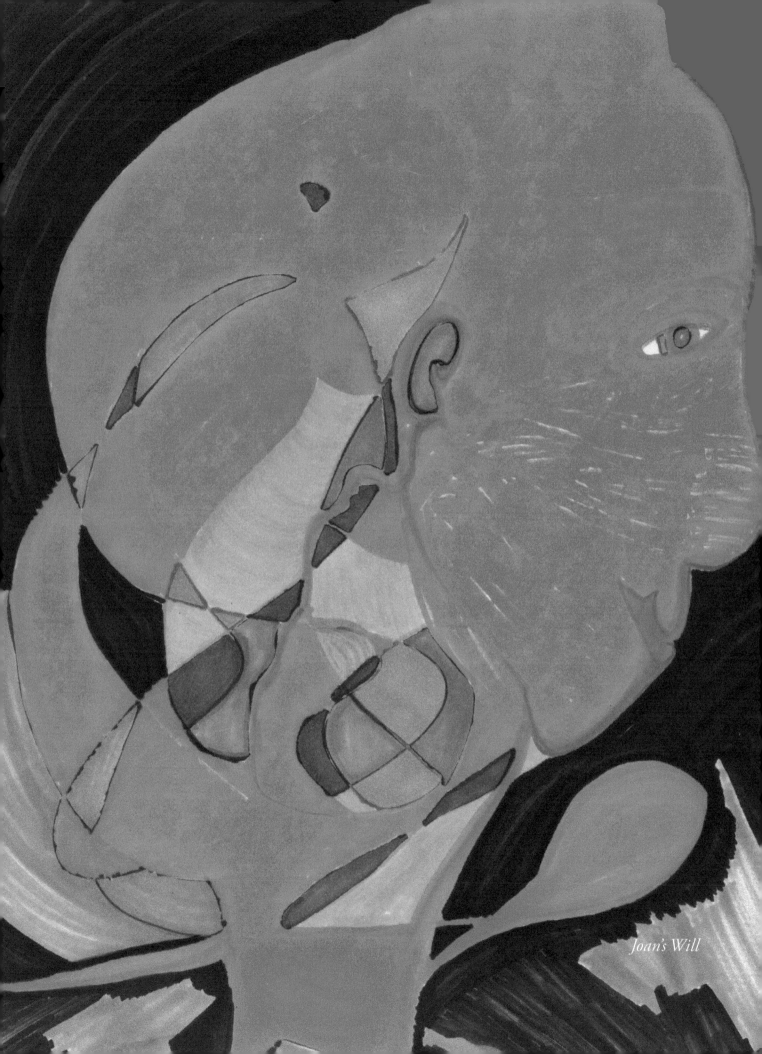

The Farmer

Walking Trees

Trap Setters

Ship Inspectors

Singers On The String

The World

Computerized People

Emotional Excavators

Thought Tracers

Ice & Wind Manipulators

Mediators

Hot Tub

Islands In The Sky

Wishing Well

Lost Fortune Lost

Red Coats

Cave Digger

The Portal

Purple Wall

Black Robe

Underwater

Broken Prince

Summer's Flower

The Dream Seeker

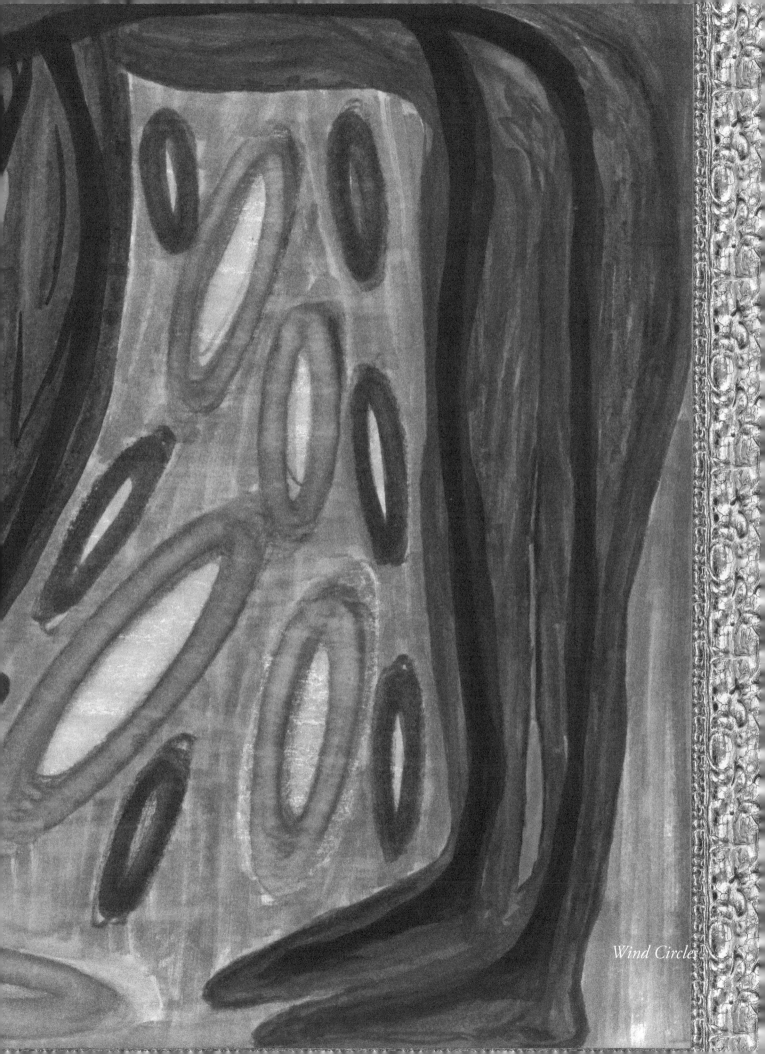

Wind Circles

Venus Rising

The Star Ship

Passengers

Electric Rain

Sea Fire

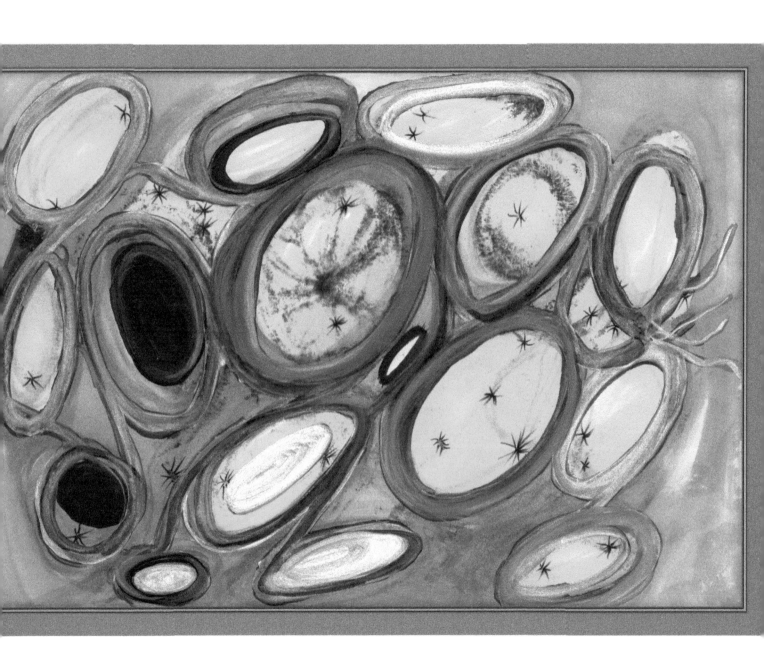

Water Seeds

Remembering

Birth Canal

The Queen's Chamber

Circles Never Sleep

Always In Space

Always Awake

Born Again & Again

The Flood

Dream Shadow

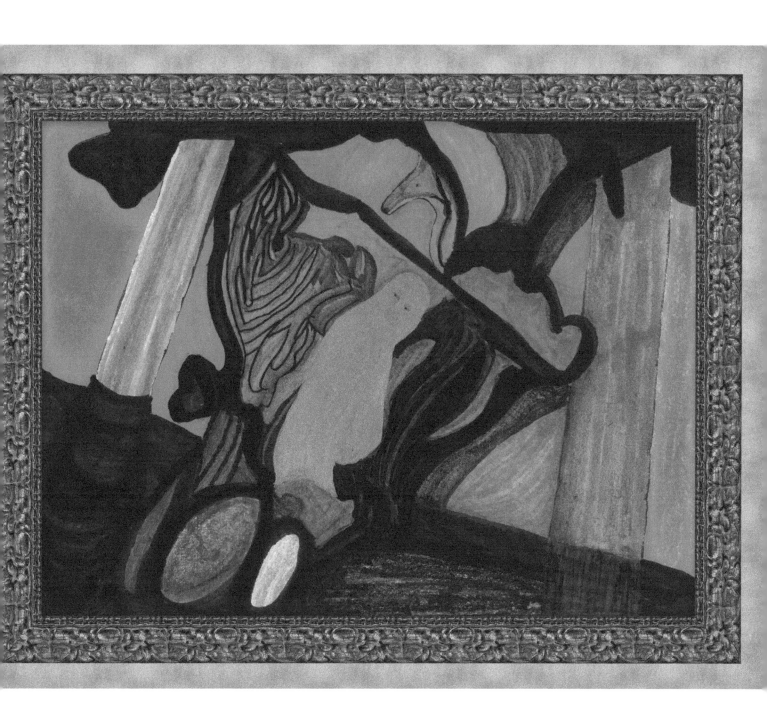

Mithras Rising

The Silken Weaver

People Of Earth

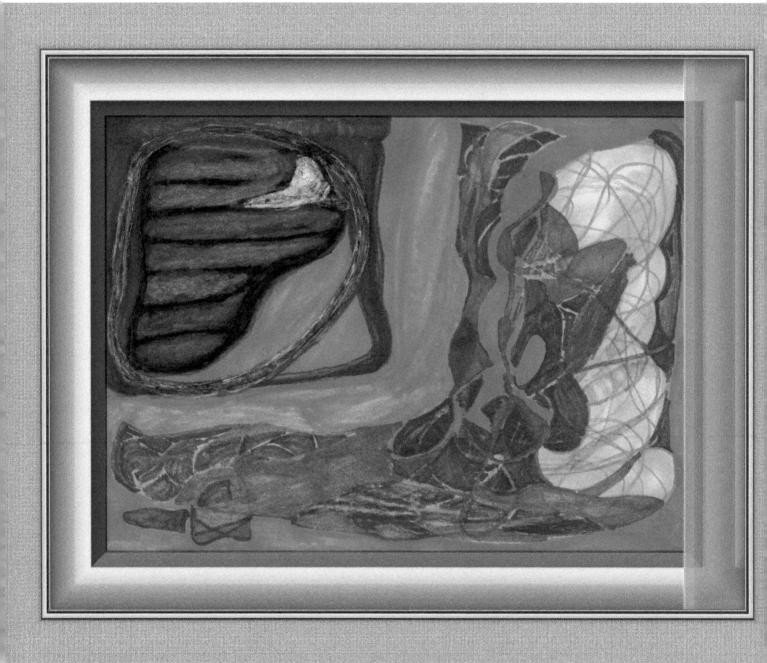

Kneeling Down To Pray

Travelers

Posted Sign

Mountain People

The Key Is Found

The Dancing Queen

Space Hotel

Peace Is Heard

EPILOGUE

By Santo Cervello

So many forces flow through our lives during each moment. Our thinking, our emotions and our desires have become electrified. The one common thread that people share is that we are human beings. We must be worthy of that powerful thread. It is the greatest honor.

GOLDEN TIME GATES
BOOK OF ART

CPSIA information can be obtained
at www.ICGtesting.com
Printed in the USA
BVHW011429280223
659388BV00006B/276